Blue

Mist

White

Rain

By

Sha Raaven

SPECIAL THANKS & ACKNOWLEDGMENTS:

My Love and Gratitude:
For those who have walked a golden path, those whom I have met along this path, and those whom which I was born into this path. To Horus, Nevio, Ferdinand & Gieves who naturally give unconditional love, Natalie, Denise, Shaman J., and Patricia Ann whose contribution is spiritually ordained. To the animal kingdom who teach us how to live life to the fullest as every minute counts. To my blood family and those related by nature & spirit. And to my ancestors who started the ball of confusion.
We have all chosen this earth journey, so until we meet again.....

Permission request can be forwarded to:
bluemistwhiterain@yahoo.co.uk

Raaven, Sha
Blue Mist White Rain

All drawings by Sha Raaven .
Cover Art by bigstockphotos.

Back cover vintage photograph taken by T. Alex.

Other photography:
Page 44 White Dove In Flight, Ackley Road Photos
Page 48 Mountains in the fog, Icefront, bigstockphotos
Page 67 Raindrop, Seriousfun, bigstockphotos
Page 99 Broken glass, Cfoto, big stock photos
Page 126 Aeroplane Night, Grafikeray, bigstockphotos
Page 130 Borrowed Light, Maarigard, bigstockphotos
Page 131 Puzzle Pieces, DanTe, bigstockphotos
Page 162 Ballet Shoes, Rixie, bigstockphotos

All other photography by Sha Raaven Photography.

First Edition Paperback:
ISBN 978-0-9558553-0-6
United Kingdom

CONTENTS

BLUE

MIST

WHITE

RAIN

WARNING

FRAGILE:
Handle With Care

Contents
Contain
Pieces
Of
A
Human
Heart

For The Spirit That Lives Within

These words are not for me or you, but
because of me and you. Because of you, I now
know me. In retrospect, you must know you to
know me.
I have taken these words from you. They are
yours. And mine.
May the cloud that shines on your light
rain to cleanse your sun

Heart

What I Wouldn't Do

I'd drink the red of the roses
To hear the pellets of snow
Fall to lay a carpet for
Your welcome

Crisp and new and original
In its entirety

I'd bathe in the golden rays
Of Daffodils
And the Fragrant clouds
Of lavender

While the hues of heather
Colour crowns like froth
As they blanket the morning

Science

Your whispering voice
Says you are not sure
Of what you are saying

Your eyes take over
They are sure that
Who they want to see
Is me

Your bitten lip
Says you need time
To form the words

Your chosen joy takes
No time and rushes
To meet my smile

Your touch says
Science is a long way
From defining
This chemistry

Far

As far away as we are close…..

I feel you

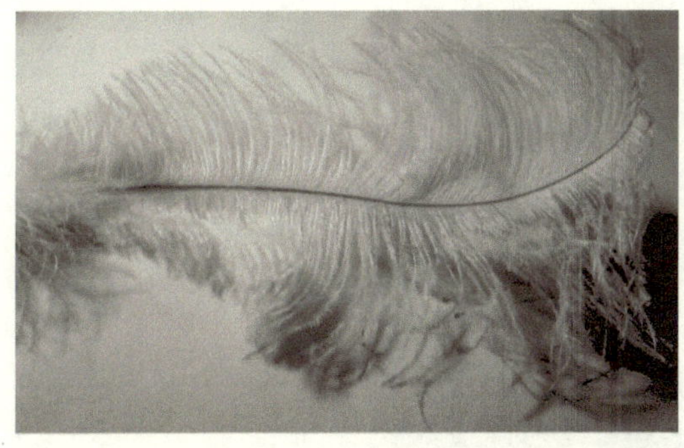

Comfort

Your closeness remains snug
Like my favourite jumper
Here to keep me warm
In this cold, cold world

Lead me to your sacred place
Where only you know the road
And the Valleys
And the way

Afternoon

A symphony of light
You speak volumes
With your eyes
They flutter when
They are full of you

An idea floats by
And following the
Wing of its tail
It's another dream
Into a fantasy
Of daydreams
You do them well

I'm There Somewhere

When I find myself away from you
And yesterday's dreams have
Become today's memories

I look for myself behind faces
I look for myself in small dark places
I look for myself in Wells Fargo cars
I look for myself in San Francisco bars

I look behind my shadow
And behind people in my shadow

And I find myself there
Standing in the back of your mind

Like time
I am aware
I am there
Somewhere

Pinch Me

He sends me love
In thoughts and dreams
It flows deeply and
Crosses the ocean that
Separates us
For now

He wishes me kind
It swims in the seas
Free from the turbulence and storm
To reach me where it's warm

He blows me his questions
So they catch me whilst I
Lay still
And when I awaken
I know the answers to send

He reaches me with his eyes
That sees the unseen
And feel the unknown
And knows what it is
To say and do to love me

He only needed to dip his toe in
To see that it was safe
I am real

Listen

If sunshine could speak

It would tell of the kisses

That we sole under its smouldering rays

If the ocean could speak

It would rave on

With the tales of our

Love that once rode its waves

If the clouds could blush

They'd muster up the deepest red

Then listen to the silence that is love

Ssshh!

Silence.......

The earth did not move
It was a single blade of grass
That swayed and shivered
When you breathed

A shadow
Captured by your secret words
Of life
Unveiled the opening
To your once familiar heart

The Air of Spring

Crisp wet day
Rain cleansing the clouds
Sun still undecided
Like the man who wrote the
HA!

Perched on my soft fluffy cloud
The virtual stranger looks over his shoulder
No need to fear
Plenty of space for you here
Are you afraid of heights?
The view from here is quite nice..................

Close your eyes. Now what do you see?

Perhaps you will tell me???

Sans the Star

And he told me
About *me*
Like this:
Satire evaded the space
I could weep in her arms for hours
She's the only one I've ever truly trusted
She fed me milky tea and scones
Her voice loved me and she saw my soul
To my best most beautiful friend
My wonderful friend I love you to the end
She brushed my hair and kissed my head
She watched as I slept
Whispered love as I wept
Took my temperature and rubbed my cough
Read the messages on my body
Painted in ink and story
Read me stories in a soft American English lilt
Threw in some French & Italian too
She held me in her soft and cuddly arms
She made me feel safe like a child
The child I had never been
Had never been allowed in
She made it perfectly safe for him
Told me to dream then dream again
Fed me fruit and croissants with coffee
And I pray to God to help me find
Someone like her
Who is nice and kind
To take me in when love's been cold
To watch me as my body grows old

She's the one I could never lie to
When the music was through
She saw the band and took my hand
No rock star roll for this pure soul
So we can't be what I would like to see
And she is kind to let me be
So kind to just be
And she knows love
And still knows me

Failing Time

The wind blew as the time began
He read the words the pen had blown
He typed me symbols spelling love
The ocean held a distance swam

I knew his past held down a tie
Baked bread and sorrow held it high
The ashes gathered round the rim
Inhaled the fumes of battered limb

Can take his love for all it's worth
Don't know for sure how wide the turf
Arms stretched to gather all in
The genuflect exorcised the sin

Forever one forever true
Make moments time fail rising dew
External cure of healthy glance
For life make way in earthly trance

Open Book Test

Deep in the mud of Glastonbury
I found a diamond in the slush
With oceans for eyes
And Waves that framed his face
How did you stay as clean?
No wonder you wiped my hands on your shirt
The rain clouded my vision
Just long enough to miss you blink
I could have sworn your eyes were tearful
Who are you?
I knew you'd take my left hand
Before you knew
So when you led me to the front of the stage
Willingly I followed
Watching your 6 foot 5 inch frame shelter me
From the rain
The bodies moved aside to let us through
Even though they were there too
You just knew
Every train ride in my brain
Searched for clues to this passenger
Destination still unknown
In the silence of speech
A place to stand and stare
And you turn me to you and hug me in close
Still silent
And when there was space between us

You spoke and told me of beauty
And that you knew me in another life
Your name sang when you spoke it
And your eyes poured deep into me
When I spoke mine
And for a day
Only 2 showed up at Glastonbury
And your hand that led me to you
And your shelter that cuddled me in
And your love you gave
And the smiles we both received from
From those around us
They knew
Somehow they knew
Or was it just so obvious
That power flower love could grow
In the mud
In the middle of a festival of sin
Christened with joy juice of the heavens
You fed me beer and tortillas and oranges
We'd both stopped smoking
So we chewed herbal gum
Keeping high on colours in our eyes
Deep in the mud
The band sang only to me
I don't remember who played that day
On the stage in front of us
Someone, many
I don't remember the rain
But I remember the rainbows

Por qué soy azul?

Couldn't tell you where these
Tears began today
Wouldn't know even if you stayed
Shouldn't try to make sense of the pain
Didn't give you time
Catch me falling idle wide-eye
Tippy toeing to hear your voice
Can't make sense of the noise
Spanish villa warm and cold
Stony floor for our old souls
Can't find out what makes it old
Won't you look and call me with your eyes?
Won't you trim the heartbeats cry?
Didn't give you time
Catch me falling idle closed eyes
Take your time

Two-Stories

It's a nice conversion to this love
The kind that makes my stomach
Ache with the ups and downs
Of swaying pink fairies

It's a nice change to this love
The kind that kicks and squeals
With joyful dance and
Surrounds itself in a
Cloak of protection

It's a meaningful love
The kind that defines
Every feeling
Every twinge in every atom of my being

You fill my dreams with
Colours and song
You fill my body with
Waves of purity and closeness
And fire

You fill my mind with visions
Of peaceful contentment
Serenity and grace
You fill my fingers with words
Of expressive joys and nuance

The Vow

My love for you was
Real and true
And how?
The scales don't lie
More good than bad
More happy than sad
My love for you was
Real and true
When I said 'I do'
It was true

Selective

I sense a beautiful mind
Looking over his shoulder
In search of a beautiful mind
Breathing easily through this month of
mystery

Viewing the selective
With selective viewing
Comfortable dwelling in the ether
for now,
Even when repeated.

I go by my gut
I live by my plexus
It shows me when to
Tells me how to do the next thing
Was meant to contact you
Still unsure why
Revealed in the end
Maybe not in this lifetime
Doesn't matter now
Don't need to know it all
Can wait for the curtain call

Like

You love me like silk

You drink me like wine

You hug me like feathers

You kiss me like Spring

Art

If I were to paint you,
I'd paint a warm heart and a soft smile.
If I were to draw you,
I'd draw a strong character and honourable deeds.
If I were to play you,
I'd play the clarinet in symphony with smooth overtones.
If I were to sing you,
I'd sing a soprano of joy and tragedy and love.
If I were to dance you,
I'd dance a bluesy sensuous freestyle with a jazzy chorus.
If I were to write you,
I'd write my words for the lovers of a diamond jewel.
If I were to act you,
I'd act a comedy of errors, a love story and a tragedy gone well.
If I were to sculpt you,
I'd sculpt a bust of beauty with the shoulders of a lion.
If I were to love you,
I just would.

If You, I Will

If you-
-
-
-
-
allow me to dissipate your darkness,

I will -
-
-
-
-
allow you to enter my light

The Walk

Trees

Thoughts tend to
Creep into that
Adjustable space
The mind

The distance between
All trees
Is my book
Of thoughts

Dove

I am so incredibly free
Not in the way birds are
But in the way that doves are

Do not ask for explanations
Just look into a clear pond

The first dove you see
Will be me

I am so incredibly free

Win

The sounds of my thoughts broke a sweat
They couldn't be ignored
Nor silenced
The colours of the letters felt
Intensely Byronesque

Dürer's ode in self portrait
And the canvas changes its pace
With the grace of a Shakespearean lead

Who comes out alive?
Who will deliver the final blow?
All tight & scrunched up,
Ready to strike a chord.

Once the whistle blows,
No game will begin.
When we change our minds,
we all win.

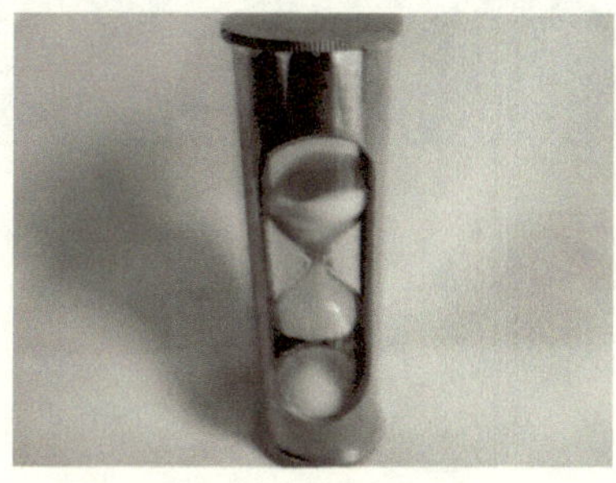

Delay Has a Speed

There is a speed with delay
That rushes to meet
Every anxiety
Every doubt
Every fear

Encasing the thought cloud above
Forced to wait
To linger
To contemplate

There's a speed with delay

Blue Mist White Rain

Stood the days by the Wintery
stairs for him
Brutal conflict stirring within
Let the tick, let the tock,
Let the ancients begin

Turning water into stone
Helping sit and stand alone
Is the obvious maker of the sea

Needing to meet the people
With integral integrity
Blue mist white rain
Showers turn the pain

Sprouting hopeless devotion
Walking barefoot meadows vast
Painting portraits peachy roses
Mighty sword offers conference
Taking life and leaving substance

The thoughts I haven't yet met
Forming new words
Whilst Freud & Jung go unsung
And Martin & Josephine dance with sheen
Having Epictetus for tea & scones
And Dali at high noon
80's retro perspective ending soon

Marcel Proust at the edge of the Indian Ocean
Succumbs Paris in the 1920's
And the concept of focus looms
Blue Mist on the endless sea
And White Rain at music's inception
Births the pulverisation of crowds

Adventurist, explorer, searcher
Warrior amongst Angels
Breathing lavender & heart
The tiger & panther greet the
Ostrich, the mouse & the owl
And the koi swam down to explore movement
As it searched the seas new ground
Where human journey's can be found

The Glory Years

This journey was hard as nails
Going backwards takes effort
Yet comfortably the memories seep into mind
The glory hoary years
When I wanted him but he wasn't there
And so the Bus Boy's filled the air
With 'Minimum Wage'
I never paid the price
Just then you took the stage
And I loved you for that
By then I was over it,
but not over you.
So I blew out Soft Cell
Who only I and Moj knew.
After all, this was late L.A.
Who fancies itself early
I sunk deep down into Romeo's Void,
And Iyall sold me magical moments of
daydream,
In sequence as she spoke for me.
I always knew I could tell some stories one day
Santa Monica was up so late
And for good reason.
They let us into the music everywhere.
Too young to get carded
And we promised not to drink.
and so we did.
No one could touch us then
We were the ones who set it all...

The standard for 80's angst.
And they followed us down the path to
One white stocking and one black one.
And Don couldn't believe it,
So he called me 'punk rock'.
I wore the title well,
With blue and green in my hair.
Such a good girl was I.
Still am, but why?
Just wanted to dance all night,
Until dawn shouted time to go home,
And I did.
Ushered by God down the Pasadena Freeway,
To the Avenues of slick turns.
Someone was watching one day.
I made it home and it's a miracle.
In at 4 and up at 7.
Managing barely.
The Kasbah rocked the Highwayman live.
And 24 at Paradise was all I could give
And Power Tools sheltered the stars into
the glory years.

No Soul

Can't shut my eyes until the ink dries
And the words have a shape
Even if they pour
From a pore with no poetry
In its soul

Safety in Falling

It was virgin snow
Piled 4 feet and glistening
Never been touched
Not even by tiny bird's feet
They know to land on
Solid ground

Erotica in safety
Mimicking cries
Pangs of anger
Lucien, even Maslow
Freud's Jung mesmerised

Waiting and watching
All in a bottle of spring
Plants stunted with growth
The scissor sharp yet dull

Pictures hang on the wall
Dangling with no promise to stay put
Still impossible,
When they are enticed.

No one would guess
For less is less is less
And things do change
And remain the same
Even having fell the distance.

There Is

There is no season
As shivering knowing settles
The closest is winter
When your thoughts freeze my heart.

"There is no reason",
as the tiny man said.
As he read and read,
never looking up to catch a scene.

There is no truth
Reached to grab in air
Turning over still undone
Bolting forward when there is none

"There is no time".
I said it wrongly and I'm treated,
Disorderly and failing
Judgements seeping.

There is no sorrow
You are there and there is here
Near is fear forever dear
Taking you and dropping me
Picking souls as souls to be.

There is no fear
Making waves for surfing near
Holding rituals dear
Holding banisters so won't
Fall and drop down forever.

There is no battle
Cold as stone and icy meadow
Follow slowly shouting please
Staying to catch the breeze.

There is no ending
20 years or decades turning
World amends and faithful
Warning.

There is no more
Live on water shut the door
Forgiven treaty cries for more
Resolution finding the good
Blessing souls as they stood still
Canopy of craving.

There is no ending
Find the cure for mad hearts
Mending and the bell tolls
Gold spending,
Buying sanity
When there is none.

Nothing Should Be Forced

Nothing should be forced
It should floooooooowww
          Like the River Thames
          Like lava from a volcano
          Like the Colorado Springs

Nothing should be forced
It should beeeeeee
          Like trees
          Like dirt
          Like air

Nothing should be forced
It should groooowww
          Like fingernails
          Like plants
          Like dust

Nothing should be forced
It should bleeeendd
          Like people and buses
          Like surfers and the ocean
          Like ray bans and Venice

Nothing
Under any circumstance
Should be forced

Pouring

October is in the depth
Then there will be no light
But that within
You will then discover
At the heart of tragedy
A core of silence
It is then appropriate to
Swim down to embrace a shadow

Ludwig

The one who has to search
and roam for words
Yet so often can be at a loss

Ludwig the poet
Longing to display on paper
the images that are packaged
in his heart

In solitude he sits alone
Yet with so many
whose pen and pad are
best friends

Friends to a heart that
Sees so much
Feels so much
with words

Watercolours

Bon Chance

The city is changing
Paris, that is.
As I walk through the West Bank
The faces are different
Cultures, expressions, attitudes
A few American voices speaking
As quietly as possible
Hoping to go unnoticed.
My little mermaid gestures to me
She wants me to try her new baked Tartines
(petit dejeuner).
And as I haven't yet had breakfast, I go.
Her husband asks where I've been.
I tell him that I've been here for 1 hour
Paris, that is.
He says I told him I was coming this weekend.
I am sure that I didn't.
He is sure that I did.
I didn't.
But he knows.
He always knows. And he's right.
He sees things that I see.
And so does she.

My French is a broken as my heart once was,
many, many years ago.
But we speak, and we know.
They feed me freshly squeezed juice and
homemade marmalade, and mango.
They want me back for dinner.

The streets are busy,
And Jean Louis appears
But only the back of his head.
He knows I'm approaching, as he turns to
greet me as soon as I reach him
We discuss his beautiful shirt .
Arm in arm, we stroll, and stop, and stroll, and
talk, and stroll.
He rubs my head like I'm a child.
And today I am.
We take refuge in the Rodin museum.
The garden has changed,
And yet it's so familiar.
If anything it's brighter.
And then I remember
That the flowers are of Summer
And the smell is of Peace.
Wanting to move but won't.
Can't.
Won't.
Finally I sit underneath 'The Thinker'.
He always shades my ever moving mind.
Ironic. Perhaps he wants to take over.
Be the first.
Be the only one who thinks,
For now.

A Parisian Memoir

I didn't mean to do it
Les Halles trampled me
And rendered me useless

So I escaped to the comfort
Of café warmth in Montmartre
The 10 francs hit the bottom
Of the saxophonists hat
With a ring that doubled its value
With sounds of wandering tourist's feet

And the nod of heads not missing a beat
Claiming Jazz as the city's unanimous treat,
Succumbed me separately.
Every step propelling me into somewhere,
Like the running in a dream.
And the screaming sound of air only.
Every coat so fair,
Every wisp of hair.
I needn't dare.

So nice not to look for anything.
Just to sit with myself and others.
Surrounded by me and others.
My frowns attract the others.
Concerned that my story was off,
For it couldn't be his story.
But it was.

Edinburgh

Your eyes fell lightly upon me
At the Edinburgh book festival
Stuck in a page of pages
Tartan scarf peeking above
a loosely fitted jacket.
Nothing unusual as usual

Care to expand on your view?
Leisurely strolling through the aisles,
Soaking up titles and author's smiles.
Not looking for anything,
and looking for something.

Is that why you followed me
after we'd bid a farewell?
Were you afraid I'd get lost?
Was my passport stamped to my head?
Did I still smell of airline food?

Just because I'm visiting,
doesn't mean I'm staying.
Anyone can out stay a welcome.
But only you can prolong a goodbye.

Bienvenue

I looked out of the window
On the Champs
Every footstep that gripped
The Élysées silent

Their coats hugged in warmth
Their hats held in thoughts

Heads turning on their laurels
To see me sitting alone
Smiles wafting their scents

The succulent salmon greeting
my tongue with an entrée.
I'd forgotten how lovely it was.

Amazing, every bite full of
Compliment.
'Oui Monsieur, merci',
To the invite of another glass
of Moet, exquisite in its body of soul

The pour, silent enough to
let your voice introduce its taste.

'Lovely, you agree?' he purrs.
'Depends on what you see?' I murmur.
'I see a chilled Moet travelling towards synchronicity', he relinquishes.
'Then what you see is indeed me', agreeing.
'VOILA! Lovely day agree?' he positions.
'Agree', I agree.

Scandinavian Savvy

She smiled with joy as she met me
Sweden and its entire wilderness
As wide as their smiles
How the children have grown
Too bad her husband's malice had shown

They took me to the casa
Her cool style living every corner
As cool as their silence
And the children acted out
Why did he have to shout?

Her face was a portrait of sadness
Trying hard not to let it show
As hard as it was to remain
How her son looked on
Waiting unspoken directions as a pawn

We shopped and sight-saw the town
Malmö having favoured quietness
As quiet as Düsseldorf at its best
How soundly the little girl slept
Sleep sneaking in as she wept

His burliness threatening and bullying
Showing me kind and his wife malice
So kind it was chillingly suspect
How the boy wanted me to leave

My arrival had stopped the chaos

Her voice raised a feverish pitch
As she made a discovery
So gone she could not see
How quickly the children hid
Pots could fly without the lid

The apologies came with a plea
She wanted to forgive him
And not fight in front of me
Her tears jerked the damaged ego
By laughing with glee
I would leave at noon you see

Then I would not see what was seen
Whatever he did he did it to her
And many others

And I could see that he didn't care
What I thought or she thought
He just wanted to eat his dinner
And scream and shout

He thinks I hate him
Because he hurt my friend
The lady who is his wife
But I won't bite
I wish them well and leave my spirit in sight
I left at noon you see

A Brass Sun

A brass sun shines on empty hats
Those who have no will to act

A sun that will give the body a colour
As true as the flesh of sunsets when they rest

Those with chain-mail suits
And laughter that excludes you
Can't fit you into their portraits

Slowly this brass sun will move
Into November
The season of nothing doing
The season where no winds blow and dreams
decay

This is another place
Where visions wither and dreams decay
Where bleak rocks keep the date
Waiting for the wisdom to come
The wisdom that could only pour from a brass
sun

The brass sun will shine like a ruby in the
night
To see where our journey's take flight

Secrets

Minute's blossom with wind
Secret smell did for it what
an immense bouquet of wild man
did for spring.

Teach song like the summer.
Tongue in dark love
has him burning immensely,
as people stagger about the blue morning.
She is full of secret smell.
Slender pronounced evening
Was building her love.

Avenue of working classes.
The page did teach the sound how
to smell the wind.
As time approached
cautiously, excitingly.
Secrets living vicariously
within their own corners.

I Dare

Turning away from the thrill
Can make you ill

He wore his eyes like glasses
And when you looked in
There was a never-ending depth
Right through to his soul

Like an eclipse
You daren't look there
The soul is now bare
Shaking its core
I dare
To look there

New Movers

Vague way of glancing toward that golden door
Give yourself credit for the thrill of adventure
Full moon to cancel the plan of the day
But nightfall unveils the ink on his fingers

He's climbing with silent footsteps
To worry
To worry
He's making his way
Toes sample the water

Intense attack of prism colour
A cloudy diversion of melancholy laughter
It's silent, yet still it pierces with the intensity of a New Mover

Pushing aside every odd
It's not like the dew has surfaced the mountains
Contact of sorts should say all
Storage of time recalls the initial

Enhanced glances
Reassure the finale
It's silent
The shadow of a New Mover

Blood

Gerry

I cannot imagine what you felt
What you thought as you knelt
Praying for freedom of your body
And of your mind and soul

Cherishing your children and their laughter
Making the most of it for this last hour
Must have been unbearable
Both the pain and the laughter

Could never have understood
Not with a 6 year old mind
And adults with minds not far behind
Who could have known and understood?

Do you believe they did their best?
Do you believe they neglected a test?
Do you think they kept us from the best?
Do you think 1966 was a testament to unrest?

You've told me how you really feel
You have forgiven yourself and everyone else
You have made up with your soul
You have helped me to come to peace and
grow old
Even though you never saw yourself old

And we can thank the South African
She helped me confront the fears

And the lovely Libran English lady
Who took me even further with my grief
That had been buried for 30 years

I blamed myself all this time
For not saying my prayers at bedtime
Thought God had punished me
Looked down and frowned
Then took my mommy

Walked around with this for centuries
Just me and my guilt and my furry
Did my penance after mass
Novenas handed out by Father John
5 Our Fathers and 10 Hail Mary's

Then Spirit showed me you and Sarah too
Smiling down at me with Ella not long after
you
She told me to take it easy for a change
And lighten up on myself and the blame

You are smarter than you know
Taking those videos that I have to show
Reminding me from where I came
Helping to take away the shame

Your other daughter needs you
She suffers from something no one knew
Not sure how or what to do
Help her to heal as you do

Responsible for our own lives without you
Something I think she finds hard to do
Never connected with her soul without you
Cannot be new
Always been there with or without you
And you knew we were different too

And I love to recall your perfume and calls
Your voice sometimes shrieking
Down those halls
'Time to eat. Come on girls.'
Your feet in socks and your hair in curls

And you sewed us up in the finest linens
With tailored coats and crisp crinolines
And shiny shoes and lacy socks
And hair that smelt of hair so new with
braided locks

Tangled with love and knots
Combing through the tresses
Didn't mind because you combed it with kind
And curled it with a southern mind

And your husband stood silently happy
First time in his life
Seemed healed from demons that almost took
his life
But fate caught up with his past
And took you away

Surely you watched as he sank into a bottle
Of depression and anger and cans of Old Style
And silence and pain and fifths of Jim Beam
And closed doors and Chesterfield's and TV
screens

And he just lost interest in life and living
And worked to pay for the house you started
And for the girls you birthed
And mourned for his mother who had just left
the earth

He cried and cried his tears of pain
And never recovered from his bruises in life
Tried to silence his pain but never regained
His interest in love had already waned
Too much pain
So much pain
Permanent stain

You watched it all, helpless in his fall
Has to take his own path and learn like us all
And every mistake and decision his own
Hardened heart carrying the memories shown

Never spoke of his father and never knew why
Then met his half brothers and sorry was I
Then I knew why he kept them a secret too
Never look for demons unless they look to find
you

Sometimes thought he hated us
Sister and I would fuss and fuss
Lost patience with us often in disgust
Sorry for that father but you know us

Left a legend in your name
Beautiful woman with lots of love to give
Made us happy with cakes and dreams
Let us live a good and happy life
The pictures are surreal
They show you in all your appeal
Can't make up for you being here
But love is real and never ending

There is no end
You are still here
And I can see you
But you know I could never say it
Not to those who are still hurting
Making it our little secret
Until now

Loving you mother through infinity
Loving your kindness and strength
Loving you mother forever more
Loving you mother
See you at the door

They Called Him Johnny

Echoes run through your veins
Blood of ancestry reign

Sonnet in fine tune joy
Sacred and meaning the boy

Frightened & weary for he is in pain
Medicines pour when no diagnosis sane

Blind in the ways of walking on water
Failing to search the survival book of disorder

Choices of mother knew downward ways
Men of the tainted unscrupulous ways

Copying her & you picked them all low
Letting them down to how far they could go

Death and its siren too loud to hear
Friction in mind to forget it would kill

Saving the grace for the one to come next
Weathering storms of her bringing her best

Caption should read of warning so near
Blessing the saved day twice in fear

Saying your grace for there's no second chance
Praying the life so she'd stay in romance

Never the ruler of fate so she went on her way
Downward the last of your sparkle to stay

Angry at God as they took her away
Happy to drown in your sacred space

Eyes down to earth so can't see arms
outstretched
Two of the girls dropped straight from the nest

Leaving them there showed a feeble mind
Crunched in the darkness as judgment would
find

Cruel is the one who ignores his fate
Pounded the heart of the girls with stake

Adults in circles with child-like minds
Holding the cards to two lives left behind

Someone to shout 'Wake Up' from your stupor
'Can't leave them here' find the key to the door

Holiness sank as the girls made their way
Fateful decisions for them in namesake

Watch as they sink into downward ways
Devil in sight with jealousy stay

Ebullient was one & determined to leave
Errant is still her crown of ease

Yammering through to find peace & calm
Pavid of his potentate ruler norm

Sickness surrounding the top of the house
Ghosts ruling the basement lot

Coffee grounds whiffing the morning bell
Chillies stinging the nostrils spell

Anchors distaff of gentle reminders
Films too hot to relish the finders

School of the science of nuns to cleanse
Novenas & rosaries exorcised the sins

Presence so felt yet distance so far
Fearing the needy girls hearts of sorrow

Thousands of chemicals leapt into lungs
Devouring the soul of a man out spun

Have you minded there are children to stay?
Have you minded your health to pay?

So both of your bodies gave in to your plea
And died a death of fateful disease

And left the two girls to fend & to mend
As adult children wearing masks of grin

And laughter became the eldest ones armour
In hiding from life to depend on those who'd
harm her

The grave may be empty you never sat down
Unless baseball was blaring for hours in sound

No more to forgive than forgiveness allows
A father remembers his faithful vows

To see you is now the same as then
Yet peace on your face the éclat wins

The love of your life holds your hand so dear
She's with you there now no longer in fear

A family of 5 includes mother's son
Who never touched the earth, the angels won

The understanding is now so very clear
The answers you give in dreams so real

And passion grows deep in love from a child
No matter how far the heart is in miles

Raking Leaves Over Cold Stones

The souls are not there
They have moved on
But the bones remain
Underneath the cold stones

If I could watch from above
I would see a vision of love
Pouring into the stones
Of many graves unknown

When I see you as you are
You are not in the ground
When I see you as you are
You are walking around

You are not laid down
You are up, alive and abound
But we go and pay our respects
To the names on the stones
As their spirits look down

DNA: Don't Know Anything

Colony of sin accompanies your gin
Gathering an army chanting,
'Going to take her down'.
Incarceration never reformed a
slithering snake.
Your lies made their way past false teeth,
A thin line drawn.
And if the jury was out
You'd still be sent packing
Demons never travel light
The old man warned me.
But not enough.
He said the man they said was
his son was 'no good'. His own words.
And his grave must be upturned.
He can now see the truth of his DNA.
And the main truth up on the big screen.
'All this time & he's not even mine'.
But he is mine. Dad that is.
And I think you know or suspect.
And it's eaten you alive.
Rotted you from the inside out,
Rotted you to the core.
That is your poison,
Among other things.
Not me.
Don't need those lecherous fiends,
Needing me for what I can give them.
Glad you lied their way right out of my life.

I thank you for that at least.
So go & drown in your sea of made up gossip,
And the fools who listen drown in treachery with you.
Still they have been warned.
And the ones who still listen will drown in their scorn.
There's no life boat here.
You aim to kill souls.
But this soul survived.
So sleep well in your bed of trouble.
You are comfortable with your serpents.
And ask your demons to save you.
And bid farewell to the good ones.

The Other One

The lady was stuck in her home
Living her life from the numbers called
Venturing out into the past
Living life and barely living

No purpose in this world
Refusing to change the already done
Letting her past keep her there
Blaming others for the world she makes

And some parents can't parent
And grown women often fail
Too ignorant so you ignore
Too jealous so it blocks a heavenly voice

And the blame is still circling
In the overhead cabin that is your mind

How long will you live on life's edge?
How long will you ask others to pay?
How long will you drop responsibility?
How long will you laugh at your state?

How long will you curse and swear?
How long will your burden bear?
How long will the distance tear?
How long will the mirror stare?

Never liked what you saw in me
Never wanted to get close to see

Never needed from me but a fee
Never loved with true heart you see

Others see but too green with envy
Others know but no help for you
Others talk about how to help you
Others keep you needing too

No light no sun no moon
No reading or museum soon
No pictures no music
All doom
Boring living inside your gloom

Never understood a lack of work
Never got why you had that smirk
Never got your anger with me
Never got why you believed a liar rather than
to ask me

Fuelled by your anger and bully
Fuelled with envy without knowing fully
Fuelled with your past mistakes
Fuelled with your hatred half-baked

Hope to see you turn the tide
Hope to see it in this lifetime
Hope you find peace and all that binds
Hope you find love in loving kind

And one day a friendship we find
And as comfortable a soul am I
That allowed the past to die
Can gleefully hold my head high
Forgave those who have struck me with lies

And some day a clear mind you gain
Through hard work you can heal the pain
But to seek that true peace you must
For it's there if you could find it in your heart
to trust.

Freedom Of Peace

Supporting the back of you
Head hunched on pillow
Eyes closed to the voices
Girls screaming for attention
Boys angry from too much
And you had none
Mum was numb
Set you aside to ignorance
Hating all women isn't fair
She represents herself
Mad at her and us
You lose without playing
Not the best move
Throw you out
Left with fear and doubt
Adult body child mind
You're finding it hard to be kind
Take your crap and sit in it
The angry ones don't get close to me
And you are no exception you see
I've no obligation to mean spirit & heart
And blood lines with me do not hold clout
It's your time
It's your life
Not mine
I hope you find in this lifetime
Freedom of peace

Queen Sarah

I never knew you on the earth
But you came to me once I was birthed
You've always been there with me
Watching me through the hard reality

With a voice that sings an angels glory
With a heart that shone heavens story
With a mind that takes us to a place
With a beautiful look in your eyes and face

Making us see the joy in all of life
Keeps me up when laden with strife
Helping me heal those stuck parts past
Telling me things only you could have

So grateful for your words of wisdom
So grateful for being able to see the unseen
I hear your singing and see you book in hand
I hear your songs singing in the heavens

So proud and happy to have your blood
Breaking the chains of generational curse
Making sure we grow in life's journey
Taking with us past life's learning

2 Angels 1 Heart

I can smell it from the car
You've made a cake for us
And Johnny brought us up

Collins and his smile
Cigar trail a mile
Laughter helping to heal mankind

Son in heavens lair so fair
All together now and memories prevail
Thanking you for kindness of heart
Thanking you for the love from the start

Memories wonderful and so true
And I am thanking you

Medicine Man

They saw you in Spain
You came with your herbs
Your hands and your cures

I saw you in Bruges
You came with your books
And your tools

They met us half way
They were sent with their
Minds to learn the way

The tepee was full
Making sweats of the demons
That makes them full

Couldn't drink from the well
Only pure of the heart
And the body to swell

Leaving past as pasts hide
And the medicines you do
Full of love with no pride

Human as we once were
Spirit as we are now
And sitting well with
Cures as medicines are

Ella

You made it OK to be a silent child
You let me play with my dolls awhile
You took me to get those shoes so dear
And wiped my tears that spilled

You gave me a clarinet to play
Hoping it would take my pain away
You baked me cookies to be Queen
And I won and waved to you & Irene

You held me as I threw up the fish
Allergic and my body wasn't used to it
You watched us dance a routine with a grin
And helped lead the girls into many a win

You gave us your time and your love
You took us to the Place with love
You gave us peanut butter cookies
Pineapple soda and root beer
And told me she was watching from above

We cannot explain how it happens
And we cannot take it for granted
That you were the one that was meant to
mother the girls who lost their mother.
And give peace to a life so frantic

I brushed your hair with sheer delight
Practiced hairstyles on your long tresses
Yet you pulled your hair into that bun
And wore cotton stripy dresses

Your son said he couldn't cope one bit
Amazing how a man can fall apart
Not at dawn but at the stroke of midnight
He could have died with his wife from a
broken heart

And then you were ready to go away
Great Angels are never meant to stay
We cherished our time on earth with you
And then no one was here to shelter us
And the ladies above were waiting for you

And when I see you in my mind's eye
Your wisdom frames your face with glee
And I welcome the knowledge you pass on to
me
And you hold me close to you
Always
As Grandmothers do

In-Lawful

I know you took me as I am
Your son was known for hurt and sin
Can't blame you for not fixing him
Took him as he was back then

Tried my best and prayed he'd mend
Nursing pain my own defence
Didn't lie about my past
He snuck in private places too fast

Won't recover from this too quick
First things first and they tend to stick
Moved and made a final step
Happiness held me as I wept

He turned into the devil as seen before
Then walked in as angel like none before
I said black and he said white
Sky was blue but none in sight

Poured the water all over me
He threw the glass that broke in pieces
He tossed the apple in view to hit me
He twisted my arm to break the bone in me

Escaped his wrath and fury finally
Meanness won't change
He's far too angry
Wonder where he learnt to be?
Couldn't just stem from being with me.

And after all these years I am safe
Then a message comes with hell hath breath
Was it fate?
Still enraged at my survival
Abuse is engraved in his words to rival
Showed me how far I have come to heal
He's still the same as he has revealed

Didn't need to know for sure before
Know now I had to close the door
I wish him well and hope for you the same
And that one day you can accept your blame

Water and Wind

Can't make it up
And there is no such thing
You never planned your exit
Not with water and wind

And you took it gracefully
Somehow I believe you knew
Or else you would have gone too
Don't believe you chose to
Go without bidding adieu

Made your statement in many ways
Left your imprint on calendar days
Loving memory of the finest of character
Legend lasting in your own time

Moving on, and up, and out
The soul knows when, without much doubt.
Accept your glory from those who know,
Love for you we're pleased to show

But I have a message to you my friend
Your work is only beginning not ending
You have your sons to heal and help
You have much work to do for yourself

Rejoined with those whom you love so dear
The man you loved and your family too
Hope you are having coffee with Ella
And gossiping about the neighbours soon

Help your family to see the unseen
Show them there is more than they know
Give them glimpses of what you can do
Help them to see you as I do

I hope you have made peace with the man you loved
His Spirit is with me from above
He has helped me along this path
And comes to me for peace
To heal his own past

It's not how you went that is remembered
But how you stayed here and lived
It's not how the wind took you away
It's not the water that made you stay
It's your love that you left behind
And a kind heart, soul and mind

Broken

Script

You live your life to a script
Afraid I might write a poem about you
Afraid that the latest episode might turn into
prose

You needn't have bothered
You don't rhyme with anything
Especially not with me
I can't fit you into prose
There's nowhere to go
Just like us
At a dead end
And here I am again
Spending words on you

I'm always drawn upwards
Towards the highest point
The highest space
I enjoy the look down
Without actually being there
Height not only clears my ears
It clears those traffic lanes in my head
And with height, there is no limit
And no end
Unlike us

And so, how did I arrive at this space?
Whilst perched on a mountain in Snowdonia
I sat on a cliff that stopped up my ears
And made me gasp for its crisp, sharp air
And took my breath with exigent flair
And I thought of everything
And everyone
Except you

Curtain Call

Woken by the fear
Asleep with worry
He burns through me in a good way
And leaves me with his happiness
It somehow translates to sadness
Imbalanced with fear
Not from him or what he brings
But from me and what I don't bring
He keeps coming back
I let him
How many endings are there to this
beginning?

Damp

Sitting in this puddle of hurt
It's damp
Cold
Lonely
Surrounded by my pain
Poured onto me
By buckets filled up with emptiness
That toppled over with one
Word

G
O
O
D
B
Y
E

How Do You Breathe?

You see the ink as white
You see the future as bright
You see the girl as dark
You see your future as parked

You take fullness of brain
No diagnosis sane
No treaty tempting fate
The blood hound not the snake

You made your mind tidy up
All obstacles and bluff
You put it all on hold
So much is controlled

You said some words of guile
Twisted package of lies
Apology short lived
A short time to forgive

A change of head and heart
An ocean between from the start
Leave last and past where it is
The energies protect what was once fear

You know your decisive mistake
Judgement from those whose work was at
stake
Flying a minute to home known
True colours where colours are shown

Measure

Too much time spent apart
Can breed contempt
Absence fonder?
Not definite
Are you sure that I
Will not grow only apart
From you
But away from you
Don't be too sure
Apart and away
Are so close

Left Is Right

You came here to love me
And I let you
You ran here to hug me
And I let you
You walked here to hear me
And I let you
You drove here to take me with you
And I let you
You lay here to keep me
And I left you

Scrutiny

In this limitless sky

In a sky

With no limits

With all that space

You read me wrongly

Maths

How can there be only two versions
When there were three people?

The End

I closed the book before we
Reached the ending
I tend to do that
Read the last chapter first

So really, I knew the ending
Before we began the beginning
And even with a bestseller
The important bits are
In the centre
That's the nourishment
Not the crust

Unions were not intended to
Be scientific
Or the greatest thing since

Your Cambridge education
Can't pick it apart
Your public school
Was out that day
This one won a prize
And freedom was the recipient

Battle Cry

I could have sworn
My heart stopped

But it's tomorrow

And I can still smell
Your hatred

Man Handle

Being faithful is not a prize

It's a given

You act as if that gives you a license

To be a fool

Just because you are only with me

Doesn't mean you have to be

But I expect you to be

And if you aren't

Then I suppose it's my consolation

For buying cheap goods

You're worth what I paid for you

But I never sold my heart

And with your manual for handling it

There are some faulty notes

'Just be faithful and you can do or say anything'

Note to yourself: DELETE

Maze

Love swept me away
From friends and family
And you
Love brightened my day
With kisses and coffee and
Dew
Love hugged me tight and
Was rough and smooth
In light
And if love knew our future
We would not be together

We Can Never Go Back

He shot words out of a canon
That was his
Weapon of mass destruction
And when they formed
An entire concept
They could break you in two

Picking up my pieces
With no help from the destroyer
Served no purpose
Except to escape
Crawling away
Hoping to be unnoticed
Drew attention like a shot
Ringing loudly in Dale Street
If only for that moment
Of Silence

I could keep crawling
And not look back
And get there faster
And I did

A May December

I've been pencilled in
I could be erased and replaced
At any moment
I want to be etched in
Permanent marker

This thing isn't make believe
It's no story book of stories
It's no pieces of dream
Glued in collage fashion

It's no rocket shot at
Speed far above and
Over our heads

It's not a true and undying romance
It's no special effect with
No afterthought

It's no use
It's no sense
It's no nonsense

It's our May December
When we're right between
Right where our middle
Feels like our end

Safety In Numbers

I heard you got married today
I don't know her
But the others do
You said she was like me
How dare you?

Who knows what you've told
Her about me?
Or if she knows your past
Back to a woman with a mind
Would that ruin it for you?

I dialled directory enquires
And like a four year old
Ecstatic over her first
Plane ride

What a thrill I received
From the recording that gave me
A string of numbers that
I will never dial

Pacifier

He tells me that he is safe
Not in the mood for debate
Wants to help for heaven's sake
Living with you is no cake bake

Trying to make you see the bleed
Turn razor sharp with speed
Time to make it all release
Don't give me phoney words to please

Noki Noki Noki san
Noki Noki Noki corozon
Noki Noki stay at home

Changed your name but not your season
Can't change your blood for that is treason
Can't change hurt and pain to reason
And your child may not have known
That you'd live with the title heathen

Want the world to fight your fight
Kick their ass and clench yours tight
Feed us you and make us swallow
Seduce us with your charms to wallow

Lead us down a garden path
Paved with anger laced with wrath
Make my stomach churn to wait
Promised passion but no release date

Draw us closer to your world
Make us see the shell and polish the pearl
Make us see your need for speed
Draw us into your den of dogs and thieves

No use to me not anymore
Sliced the balls and ended your score
Stopped on 4 but maybe more
Babies' momma's not so sure

Don't know shame only fame
Don't cry much because it's in vain
Don't leave scars, you just leave pain
Don't need much to play this game
Don't know shame, you only blame

Said the addict is too static
Systems work within the panic
Works if worked, and you can work it
Take the frame and make it fit

Said I'd never do it again
Said no alcoholic, no junkie, no sin
Said he'd have to be clean to win
Said he won't seduce me to him
Said I'd throw away fun to the wind
Said I'd die bored but at least I'd have lived
Said he'd never get into this soul again
Said it would never happen

Said he took me and held me with care
Said he squeezed me to what I could bare
Said he opened my heart with his spear
Said he told me he loved me in fear

Said he captured my soul all in
Said he kissed what was left of my sin
Said he drained all my fire within
Said he came to conquer and win

Said he held me and jelled me in slow
Said he whispered the words and felt it flow
Said he knew what he needed to know
Said he came to see all of the show

Said he wanted to get what was his
Said he tried to make light of this biz
Said he dreamed and a dream it is
Said he came for what was his

Do you want me to go I can do?
Do you want me to stay with you?
Do you want me to call you too?
Do you want me to love you too?

Said he'd never fall off his binge wagon
Said he'd work it when he was flagging
Said he'd done all that and was through
Said he knew all that I knew

Said he just wanted to be normal
Said he struck the match paranormal

I say you got something from me
I say all you wanted was to be free
I say you do what it is you do
I say a friendship strong,
But this love is through.

Sweet Guitar

Uncanny
A DVD and me
On the off chance
Or was it?
And it happens again
I see him there and flashback
He stood out then
But it is years later that I see him
Really see him
And there he is
All bright and shiny
Pouring sugar all over his guitar
Lapping it up like he means it
Claiming that melody as his own
And it is
And he is LAPIMEDIPADIA
What I hear is orgasmic
He knows what I mean
Because thanks to Gates
I've told him
And he's thanked me
I see their light
But I don't know if I want to anymore
It brings sheer joy at first
And then the sadness begins
It conquers my head
They all succeed
They must

They trust what they have
They hear it and they listen
And it happened the exact same time
Last year
And two years before
Different source
Same glow
And I sent him love
And he received it
And it made his day, his year, his life
And he phoned, but got laryngitis
So he hung up
Never said much
People don't do that these days
And after him
Another glow
Albeit dimmer this time
Still I got through
I saw it and I told him
And he gave me a word
A 'Ha!'
Didn't expect more from this one
That light in him had burnt out long ago
He's already used a few of his lives
There can't be any left

But they see what they have
They trust it
I see it too

ABC

As your friend I tell you only truth
You are trying to move on
I can see that
And I wish you luck
She's drowning in fear
And making you bleed to the death

I know you feel it
I see your clenched fist
You saw it coming too
You knew it was your stop to get off
And so you did
You just forgot to stop the train first

She wanted to keep going
Even though it was empty
Empty of love
Empty of passion
Empty of you

You couldn't lie in that life
It was enough to pretend for a living
You want to go home
and be the truth

And so you should be allowed to do just that
Point X to Point Z
Y couldn't be easier

Your passion was x-rated
But not enough to agree on the ABC's
The gift of a child is magnetic
But not enough to glue you together
Opposites repel
And so you did

Don't expect her to wish you well

Disgusted Disguise

You managed to sell me you
And I bought in
The whole package
Without seeing it up close
Without a guarantee
Without a license to operate a selfish man

And with all new things
Waiting for arrival
There is delayed gratification
I only have the picture to remind me of what I bought

And it's all good from a distance
It might be different up front
You might not be actual size
This I won't know until you arrive
Meanwhile I will just get substitutes
To fill the time in place of you
And when you arrive
If you are not what I expected
In the flesh

I can always return you
No questions asked
If that is allowed
After all
There was never any guarantee

Seat With My Name On It

This is my seat
It definitely has my name on it
Stockholm was waiting for me
It waited for 4 hours
And greeted me just like before
With open arms and a seat
With my name on it

Who agreed to meet here?
Was it I?
'Twas not! It was you
But I agreed because I've
Missed this seat
The seat with my name on it

The lattes are getting cold now
Not much left to say
How many times can we end this?
How many goodbyes form a wave of a hand?
My friends wanted me to have dinner
With them
But you chose to meet here
And I agreed
If I had been late
I would have missed the seat
With my name on it

So why are you so sad?
You chose to meet here
I wanted to text you

To easy-mail you
Then you wouldn't see my eyes
As I sit in this seat with my name on it

This seat is sturdy and reliable
But is it sad like you
So you sit on the edge
As of you are waiting to go
Uncomfortable in this repeat performance
I sit back comfortably in mine
It owns me after all this time
After all, this seat has my name on it

Targeted Territory

The sting stung differently this time
It still hurt
But the tears bled
A different shade of feeling
One that lacked the ingredients of the last
recipe for pain
The tears flowed few and short
Squeezed tight as if measured
And not by much
It stung differently this time

Maybe because it struck in new territory
Still in the same region
The heart area
Miles and miles of territory there
But only a portion felt the tremors

Trying to pinpoint it on the map
I know it was fear
Fear of what?
Fear of you

I don't know who they are
These last two who knew you
But they took a piece of you
So you showed up broken
Pieces missing and puzzle unsolved

It's hard to wait
Even when I know all about the 'whys'

Yet fear keeps me waiting
Still trying to pinpoint the territory
And why it has changed
Expected it to change
Couldn't stop it coming
You are you
And you will do what you do
You come first to you

Head hurts now
Developing pictures in the dark room
Of my brain
When it's dim it hurts
No strength and no gain
Squinting to see
Just pain
And it's different this time

Breath

How thoughtless of you

To put on airs

While I was still breathing

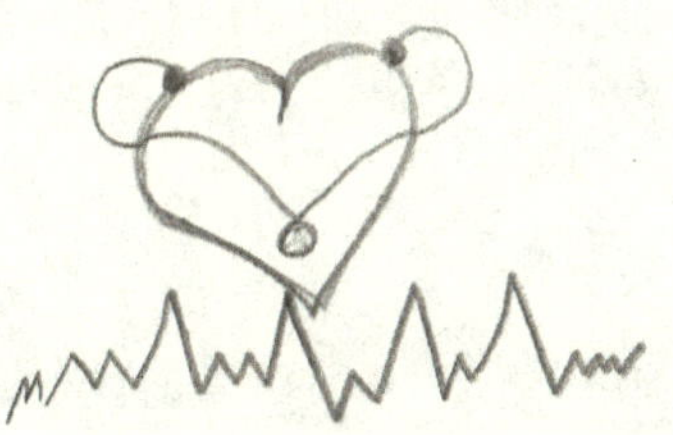

View

The sun is here!

Tears move aside

You are blocking my view

Pieces

Thought

Fraction of time spent
Mind manoeuvring
Through alley ways
Some gutter balls

Sliced into thought dimension
Fantasy orientated
Free-lance dancing eyes
Creating images
Only through dreams

Waves of current flowing
Through veins translucent with
The juice of age
Life cycle

Mountains peak to heights
Of outer limits
Walls of brick surrounding
Inner thoughts
Trying to escape

Through mouths of glass
That cut like swords into hearts
Made of steel

Neon expression
A cellophane clone
Of mime gesture

Magnetic occurrences
That connects life and love
With wonder

How thought enters the mind
Or
How the mind enters thought

Temperance

Hastily seeking the question
The answer is the one
With the patience

The Tenant

I don't mean to stare
But I'm stuck, stagnant, stalled.
You see, from its inception
Just above the arch of your eyebrow
A well-drawn line takes up residence

And like exit 5 on the 405 freeway
It deliberately curves, and I can't avoid it
I'm drawn
Like the line that drapes and shelters a nose
That only a 90210 postcode could house

And I would bet Mrs. Disney's dinner
reservation
That it was born of roots firmly anchored
In the curiosity of a 2 year old
That dug its heels in
The kind that digs in at disappointment
And love taking the next plane
And rejection undigested

It must have debuted when the best man
Started his spiel
31 years of silently bubbling under
So that you wouldn't bubble over

I suppose it talks to itself at dinner
Or maybe its entertained by the other worries
Could get real territorial
Can't allow other lines in, you know

Might have to stop them in their tracks
Even stunt their growth

'I'm the main man here. I *own* this forehead.
This is my neck of the woods
Don't even *think* about it'

It's on the move and making an approach
Just about to greet your grey
Gently introducing itself to your left temple

Could just stay there
Moist, warm, cosy
Receives an affectionate wipe now and again
Judged by others but usually respected.
And never mistaken for decoration
The end of the road
And the greys have it.

It's worked hard to secure its place
Amongst the other staring features
All gathered to tell your tale

Its pointing upwards does not console me
This clueless clue has stumped me
Will it continue on its travels?
Or just deepen its already trodden path
Will it retrace its steps, perhaps deterring off
into unknown territory?

I don't mean to stare
But I'm stuck, stagnant, stalled
You see, from its inception
Your grey hairs drop anchors deep into your earth

And grey was never so black and white

Practice

She saw the dreams in her head
As if on wide screen
And stepped into them
Every so often

The smell of smells
The air of airs
Tasting the air
Feeling the joy

She saw him in Technicolor
Felt him in Dolby
Heard him in surround sound

He was in that space
And that space was in her head
He will never know
About the head or space
And that is why there is no remote

And just for now she presses pause
That connection remains
That realm of divide
Space and the moon that rules
The season of long acres
And still touch down in reality soon

Peeling

I had to let her go
She was a scab
Hardened by life's
Curve balls
Hitting her so hard
That she froze in time
Stayed right there
Where the first ball hit

And each time I tried
To peel it away
It stiffened into
A defensive block
A boarder

Gripping more firmly to her skin
Covering her like a
Protective blazer

She built bricks of solid words
And forced smiles around her
For protection
Words that hit others as hard
As the curve balls
That hit her
So hard they
Froze in time
Or shrunk away
Vowing never to see her again

They hated her
Fired her
Sued her
Put her out
Ignored her
All the while
Hardening the scab that gripped
Firmly to her
Never letting go

Her words poured with jealously
Sarcasm
Resentfulness
Anguish
Hurting others as much as she could
Because she was hurting
As much as she could

She became an embarrassment
To her country
Her race
Her gender
Her species
She blamed the scab for the scab
Which came first?

And so it stayed
Wrapped around her
For the whole world to see

A protective meanness
A genuine disgust
Of herself, of you, of me

I let her in several times
Into my space of fluffiness
Wonderment
Love
I gave her nourishment
Of hugs, words, angels
And fairies

She greedily sucked them
From me
Happily draining my essence
Aiming for the core

Seeing my abundance of life
Pointing to my death
At points to the universe
Blinded by my protective light

So blinded she didn't recognise
My own skin that was once a scab
But is now a light of love
So blinded that she struck out to stop me
To wound me
To hinder me

It bounced off me and hit her
You cannot scab where a scab
Has already been
And there she was
Wearing a wig that resembled a scab
Hunched over
Walking with a limp
Bowled over by the weight
Of the scab that had settled
On her head
In her brain

In a designer coat
Taken from those who had
Nourished her
Those she tried to bleed dry
With legalities

Barely standing, dressed for the
Monster's ball
Still speaking of God & prayer
Yet trying to give me a spell to hex & curse
And drain me of money
To drain me
Of me

It bounced off me and hit her
Its hard to harm those who harm none

But I gave in and sent her paper
Worth money to use to barter
And then she showed her scab

So I let her go
My light sent her a light
And wishes her well in light
And a pleasant removal

Thinking Women

He thought women were
Like men
And he searched for one
To use and throw out again

The woman who would turn his
Melody into a song

On a train
On a street
In the park he longed to meet

The woman who would keep him afloat

He forgot to check
So when he met a woman
Who was unlike any woman or man

She used him
Then threw him out again

He should really think again

Backdrops

Dancing Angel

OK so you know
I don't mind that you know
But you only know what you know
And that's not everything

OK so you think
I don't mind that you think
But what you think is what YOU think
And that's not all of it

Why not listen
But not to yourself this time
To others who know
They know what you don't know
That must be hard for you to know

Where did you learn to look down?
Not from your roof but from your pedestal
Can't imagine it's a good view
And I can tell you it's not from here

Do you want to know what I think?
I think you think you know
You don't know everything
And the truth is everything
Once you hear other's words
Your everything
Will be nothing
And that's what I know

Keith

Your story ended abruptly
I'd only just started reading you
And if I hadn't been interrupted by distance
I would have kept on reading

You let me into your chapters
Your verses of struggle and ego
The kind of ego that stacks up mistakes
And stands on fear

I couldn't have cared less what you did
As long as you did it with me
But you know the way I live
And I always live freely

You were what you were meant to be
And that is hard to believe
I know it's true for you
Still surprised at your outcome of blue mist

Your curly dark hair
And cotton candy scent
Your pimp walk mimicking confidence
Your laughter that draped me
And your knack for getting away with
everything

Didn't know how much then
But your father's dread held you
And you rebelled
And gloriously too

Your Creole skin a testament to the Bayou Bay
And the music that blasted from your room
Me with Zeppelin
You with the Dramatics
Little did we know
Just how little time you'd be able to listen

And that Summer of '76
Your eyes reminded me of the Mississippi
All dark and muddy and full
Yet dangerously deep
And I knew it was risky to jump into your
space
No one could have saved me

So you dangled yourself from a safe place
Just enough for me not to drown
And in your room
We felt the safety of the stars
Even though it was a kiss
It saved me

You were my rock star
My love from afar
My little friend from a childhood so free

Our friend took you away
Left us all in shock
He fought his country's war
And came back ill
And his brain lay dead in psychotic dread

So on the 12th of the 3rd month
He raged and pointed a gun
And took you, from you
From your mom, dad, and sisters too
And from me
19 years and you were through

The news rang out
And they told me you had gone
And that summer said it all
And even though we only talked
It was long overdue

And my tears fell hard
Remembered when you took up for me

In music class
You were sweet and loving
And the girls loved you
And you loved me

Remembered when your sister gave me lollies
And change to buy the candies
She let me in
Because of you

You were my rock star
Never had to worship you from afar
And it all went so terribly wrong
You played life to your song

How could you get life so wrong?
And me so right?

Sunset & Vine & L.A. Wine

Nothing's changed
It's just like I left it
People going everywhere
And ending up nowhere

Searching for a star down there
When they are all up there
Too flaky to look up
For fear of running into other egos

And that must really hurt
To believe you are the best
And then be put to a test
And then forced to wait on their guests

And whatever it means
It must be something in the Californian air
That clogs up the minds of all those who
breathe it
And then takes their hearts to a place of no
return

And is it any wonder why they turn to flake?
Airing their brains to smoggy content
Feeling their way through short skirts
Lying their way to audition a soul

And the story goes on

Never want that tag on my toe
But you will always know who
Has been tagged here
Their steps become heavier during their 9-5's
It's their only way to survive
And not mentioning their time to lie down and die
But the drummer plays that song for so long
And now he's tired of his own tone

Come one come all to the place of mind bog
Selling life as it's meant to be sold
And you have never been so bold
Sink or swim
The flaky jump in

I hope to see you healthy and good
But this town could not be misunderstood
So I'll settle for what you become
Be it survivor or undone

The Rainbow's bar is packed tonight
And the actor turned up with tow in sight
The rock god laid his feet on a table
Looking for love from the brain disabled

And they all found it here
The city that dreams a dream and catches a cat nap
So full of itself in all its gold

Just because you catch the most sun

Doesn't mean you're always going to be fun
It's hard to imagine real people in their homes
You only hear the muffled laughing tones

And it's hard to believe I once called this place
home

Yet the beautiful ocean is always in sight
Pacific waves dance as the ever hopefuls roam

Her Sister

You came to me as you were

And your beauty of heart is pure

Then you drowned in her shadow

Could see it but it didn't matter

Family is strong and friendships tighter

Can't blame you for her laughter

Karaoke mind and new wave view

Love you friend and friendships true

Hope to see your lovely smile

Clear soul light and always loving smile

Doesn't shadow you with her light

Another Kelly

When you fell backwards in the Slug
We roared with the laughter of 6 year olds
And your glass never spilt a drop of lager
That is your way

When you fell asleep on top of a car in
Portobello
We repeated the story for years
Only because you woke up missing one doc
martins

Could only happen to you
When you laughed we would laugh
Your world was infectious
And we will always be asking the same
question
'Are those eyes real or green contacts?'

When we walked to Oxford Street
We smoked my brand of Dunhill's
And we talked about the 2 Paul's

Your one was causing havoc
My one was drinking wreaking havoc
We should have stayed away from both

In the words of D-boy
'Bad Move'
'You got a pen?'

And then we fell off our seats
Until the Iranian walked in
And we asked him the time
And he replied like a recording,
'Exactlyyyyyyy one o'clock'
Angelo's held our table
And we gladly held court
And the Grolsh fell past our lips
While the smoke filled the air and our lungs

And with a card behind the bar
The drinks poured and the calamari soared
And Sonia told us her story

Of how Alex was in trouble in Thailand
And at the point of no return and trouble
And we were sad

We liked Alex
And then he walked in
And we could never believe Sonia again
And we laughed and so did she
And so did he
Our substance was shaking

And we knew how to have fun
Until the dating had begun

'Bad Move'
But we laughed anyway
And D-boy saw a movie
'A River Runs Through It'
But you had to hear him say it
It's all in the way he says it

Quick, fast and hard
And we laughed
And things could turn sour
Was it the Sunday Times in the pub?
Or my engagement to an idiot in the pub?

It's like the chicken and the egg
But Sonia saw in me what I needed to see
But I could not see it then
And that's OK
It would all mend

And it did
You were such a part of me
The 3 Amigos you see
And then it ended
Where are you?

Fallen away
Kept in touch for some time
And even came to stay
But never keeping the gate open
So you may find me

And that would be cool

That would be choice

Duuuudddee!

That would be so COOL!

Secret Mission

Today, I heard that you'd passed away
The memories came flooding into view
It could not be you
You had so much more to do

But we take it as it comes
And I know your gold was none
Yet your heart wore sleeves for fun
And I loved you as you were

I wish your children well
And hope they know their mother well
Because she was a gem of a girl
And danced with elegance

You are alive in my world
I hope you visit me often
And listen to my tunes
And watch over my guitar man
He needs the sympathy
That I can't give him

I hope you see my heart as it is
I know you know I did my best
As your friend and to all the rest
I pray for your healing at best

When I see you again
Your soul at rest
We can dance down that line

And laugh at the man
Who told me I was too new wave
How can you be there before him?

Makes me think of life as grim
But kick-starting a revolution
'ain't gonna change a thing
You're there now and having fun

And your secret mission
Now that you've chosen to accept it
Is to give your children great wisdom
Your smile & your kindness
And to keep the bad ones away

I miss you little angel
Always knew you were true blue
This life has sharper turns unknown
And were met with golden hue

Ballerina

He danced and he danced
And walked head held high
And sauntered into a magical world
Of pointed toes and wistful bows

And the stage was the home
For years to come
Smelling of freshly washed floors
And good reviews

And you tried to tell me
A difficult thing
A thing a friend shouldn't hear
Whilst standing in the wings

This friend had sorrows
And sticky tape
The friend had learnt to love lost & hate

But you came through it well
And you leaped into mountainous art
And so I can be proud
That you danced a dance of kind

And I hope you can trust
That when you find him
The difference lie
In knowing and leaping
With wide eyes

Bus Pass

Your pain was masked in smart aleck tone
Laughing at your own jokes
And making me do the same

And when we walked into Paradise
We wore the glasses of fame
Incognito and everyone interrupting us
Looking to spot the real ones

Someone was in the VIP
And we knew them
But we couldn't be bothered to go
Instead Larry ate his dinner
And we did too

Making appearances
Recognising us as we are
Not on the bus as you joked
But in my red beetle
Which was so LA

And we danced when asked to dance
And we sat when asked to dance
And we didn't care who asked
Both of us had enough of him
Telling us what to do
And who to do it to

I promise you this
I didn't know J was going to put the pie in
your face
But it was funny all the same
And who was to know
That my caped crusader
Would spread her legs for the world
And become public enemy
And be ousted for her no good

Babysitting was supposed to be easy
What happened there?
Not responsible for that
Did my best

And then you told me you were sick
And those chemicals did the trick
Never penned you for that
But no judgement
You got back on course
So this is the horse race
To stay alive

Your life is getting better
Thank goodness for that
But how can we ever go out
In sunglasses again?

Strummer

Feeling the absence of a heart grow fonder
Feeling I want to get closer to him now
Feeling him play the way he knows how
Feeling a song well up in his heart

Easy to see us finding our way
Easy to see 'we' as wings find play
Easy to show the likeness we face
Easy to please us when we're in this place

Whatever You Say

I don't profess to save you from me
You picked this time to find me

But since you are here
Let there be no beginning
And no ending

And whatever you see
Is in you
And whatever you do
Is your truth

And this is mine

www.ingramcontent.com/pod-product-compliance
Lightning Source LLC
LaVergne TN
LVHW090952080826
845145LV00003B/980